A Gift For

Lisa

Love, From

Mom

May 14, 2006

A Mother is for Always

Gloria Evangelista

Nashville, Tennessee

A Mother is for Always

Project Editor: Kathy Baker

Art Direction/Design: P. David Eleazar and Khris Mabry for
The Eleazar Group, Nashville, Tennessee. www.eleazargroup.com

ISBN 1-4041-0058-X

Printed and bound in the United States of America

www.jcountryman.com
www.thomasnelson.com

This book is dedicated to

my *mother*, my *always*

and to my *children*, for *always*

Only a Father with so perfect a love for

His children allows a mother to be for always

He has offered His hands . . .

so when I am gone, I will be able to roll your sadness

into a ball and hurl it, like a meteor in space, far from

your heart always

And the use of His palms . . .

to catch your tears and pour them into a stream where

salmon spawn so when the eggs hatch you will see

joyful new life

And His
infinite grasp . . .

to gather the darkness that
surrounds you and fill it with
light so you will never be lost.

The flowers appear on the earth;
The time of singing has come ....
—Song of Solomon 2:12

He has extended the power of His majesty . .

to awaken the springtime grasses for you to frolic in their
coolness, and to deliver fragrant showers so daisies and
daffodils will rise to greet you always

And the wave of His arms . . .

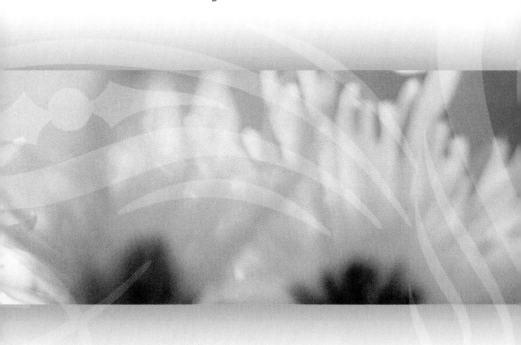

so I may send breezes to tousle your hair and ruffle
the folds of your thin cottons

to weave memories among
the pattering raindrops and
refresh the faith in your bosom.

Now faith is the substance of things hoped
for, the evidence of things not seen.
—Hebrews 11:1

He has dispensed the artistry of His eye . . .

so I may position the sun of your summer to fall

upon your face and make it golden and alive

And the wonder of His presence . . .

so I may sparkle from the sunlit dust that floats around you and rise from the sage and rosemary scents of boiled soups and roasted meats, always there to shield your eyes when the future reveals itself too soon

And the command of His voice . . .

to instruct crabs to script secret messages
as they scurry across the sand

And trumpet my love
across the sea waves,

crashing them upon the shore
so you can still hear the music
of my heart.

I will never leave you nor forsake you.
—Hebrews 13:5

Only a Father with so perfect a love for His

children allows a mother to be for always.

He has continued to love and sustain me . . .

so I may continue to love and

sustain you, always.

He has employed His breath. . .

So I may whisper through the words of others,
not to unravel mystery but to spur you to
contemplate the incomprehensible, for this
is the challenge of being human

And to dance the leaves of autumn

in circles about your feet to tease
and excite you, so you may become
ripe with possibility and things that
have never been.

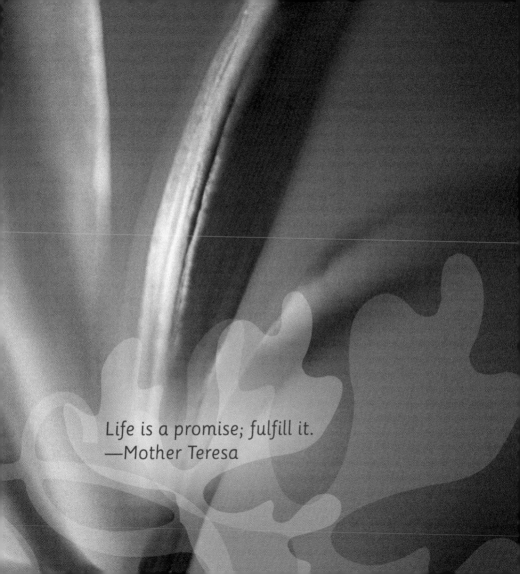

Life is a promise; fulfill it.
—Mother Teresa

He has infused the earth with

His glory and gestures . . .

always there among embroidered cornfields,
turning the vine's flower into a bright orange
squash to decorate the season of your fall

And He has instilled His spirit in me. . .

so I may instill His spirit in you

when prayers go unanswered

and songs go unsung.

And in evenings,

when church bells ring, if you are very still,
you will hear me calling, for I shall miss you, too.

To everything there is a season,

A time for every purpose under heaven.

—Ecclesiastes 3:1

Yet you should think of me and smile. . .

so I can touch the laugh lines etched

into your face and smile back

From birthday ribbons you wrap with fingers
that move as mine and the milk mustaches of
your children and their children,

Remembering always . . .

that as I am a child of God,

you are a child of God,

nothing more, nothing less

Never lose the opportunity
of seeing anything that is beautiful.
Beauty is God's handwriting.
—Ralph Waldo Emerson

And with Him beside me . . .

I will join the robin in song outside your window

and wave from the arms of willows, and trail

a fragrance of contentment as dusk bathes

the earth in candlelight

And when you sleep . . .

I will borrow *feathers* from His angels' wings and tickle your cheek with night kisses, and leave love on your pillow so you will always have enough

And wrap my arms around your dreams. . .

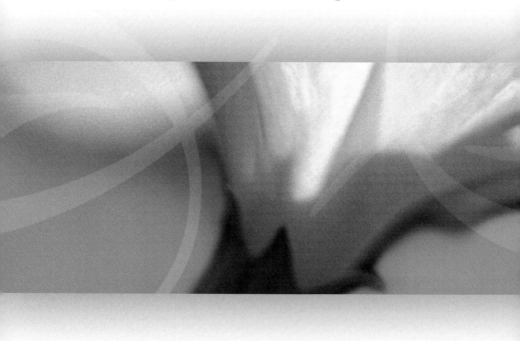

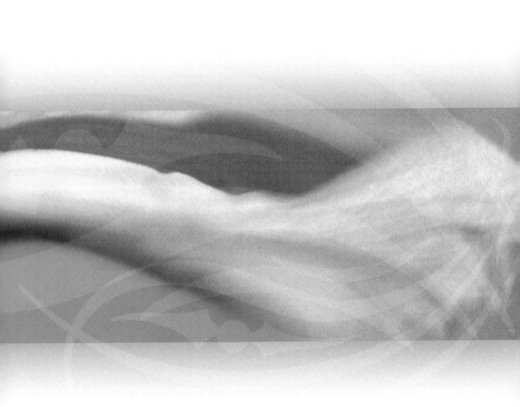

And when you awaken I will take the dreams
with me so they will be safe.

As He nourishes me,

so shall He nourish you. . .

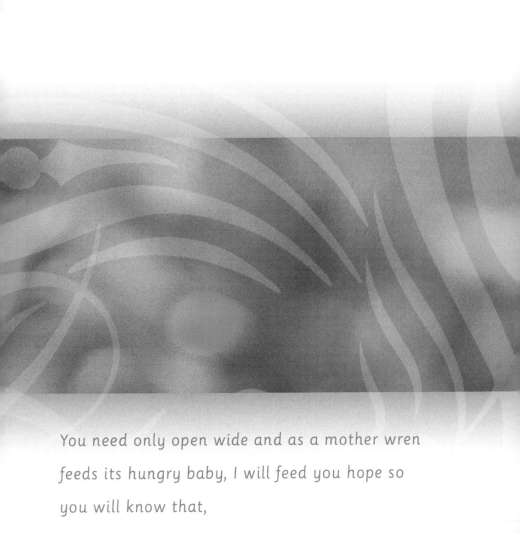

You need only open wide and as a mother wren
feeds its hungry baby, I will feed you hope so
you will know that,

Although all that
is left of me is you,

all that is left of you
is everything.

More things are wrought by prayer
than this world dreams of.
—Alfred, Lord Tennyson

And at those moments when
you stand victorious. . .

turn your face to the sun and feel

His warmth upon your cheek,

And together we will glide
and magic-carpet-ride. . .

on the winds of your life and

maneuver hills and fields of heather,

And *feel the magnificence*

of one another no matter where each resides.

I remember my mother's prayers,
they have always followed me.
They have clung to me all my life.
—Abraham Lincoln

And in the winter of your days,

curled fireside with chocolate's steaming cup and stories

told to your young, bow your head and give thanks.

And I will curl beside you as the smoke rises

from your chimney top and thank Him too,

feeling very blest that He gave me the opportunity

to have you, and grateful that He has given

you the opportunity to still have me,

Her children rise up and call her blessed.
—Proverbs 31:28

For only a Father with so

perfect a love for His children

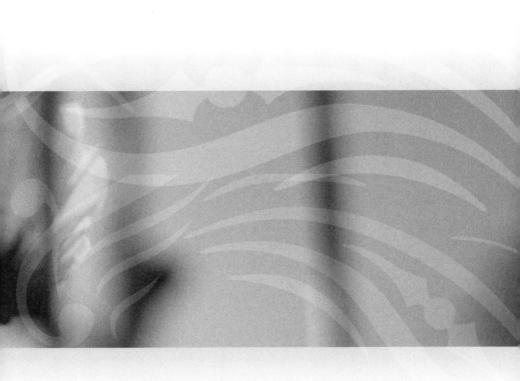

allows a mother to be for always. And although each
of us walk but once through a lifetime, we can remain
forevermore with Him

And someday far and someday near,

when the grains of your hourglass are few and all

the words of your life sprawl across the heavens,

I will be the star that you come home to.

For as no mother so loved her children,
no Father so loved His.